It's My Body

Arms, Elbows, Hands, and Fingers

Lola M. Schaefer

Heinemann Library
Chicago, Illinois

© 2003 Heinemann Library
a division of Reed Elsevier Inc.
Chicago, IL

Customer Service 888-454-2279
Visit our website at www.heinemannlibrary.com

Designed by Sue Emerson, Heinemann Library; Page layout by Que-Net Media
Printed and bound in the United States by Lake Book Manufacturing, Inc.
Photo research by Jennifer Gillis

07 06 05 04 03
10 9 8 7 6 5 4 3 2 1

Library of Congress Cataloging-in-Publication Data
Schaefer, Lola M., 1950-
   Arms, elbows, hands, and fingers / Lola M. Schaefer.
        v. cm. – (It's my body)
Includes index.
Contents: What are your arms and hands? – Where are your arms? – What do your arms look like? – What's inside your arms? – What can you do with your arms? – Where are your hands? – What do your hands look like? – What's inside your hands? – What can you do with your hands? – Quiz – Picture glossary.
   ISBN 1-4034-0889-0 (HC), 1-4034-3478-6 (Pbk.)
   1. Arm–Juvenile literature. 2. Hand–Juvenile literature. [1. Arm. 2. Hand. 3. Human anatomy.] I. Title. II. Series.
   QM548 .S345 2003
   612'.97–dc21

                                 2002014735

Acknowledgments
The author and publishers are grateful to the following for permission to reproduce copyright material:
pp. 4, 8, 20 Robert Lifson/Heinemann Library; p. 5 Jose Carillo/PhotoEdit; pp. 6, 9, 12, 13, 14, 15, 16, 17, 21, 22, 24 Brian Warling/Heinemann Library; p. 7 Left Lane Productions/Corbis; p. 10 Custom Medical Stock Photo; p. 18 CNRI/PhotoTake; p. 23. row 1 (L-R) Custom Medical Stock Photo, Collection CNRI/PhotoTake; row 2 Brian Warling/Heinemann Library; row 3 (L-R) Collection CNRI/PhotoTake, Brian Warling/Heinemann Library; back cover (L-R) Brian Warling/Heinemann Library, Collection CNRI/PhotoTake

Cover photograph by Rolf Bruderer/Corbis

Every effort has been made to contact copyright holders of any material reproduced in this book. Any omissions will be rectified in subsequent printings if notice is given to the publisher.

Special thanks to our advisory panel for their help in the preparation of this book:

Alice Bethke, Library Consultant
Palo Alto, CA

Eileen Day, Preschool Teacher
Chicago, IL

Kathleen Gilbert,
Second Grade Teacher
Round Rock, TX

Sandra Gilbert,
Library Media Specialist
Fiest Elementary School
Houston, TX

Jan Gobeille,
Kindergarten Teacher
Garfield Elementary
Oakland, CA

Angela Leeper,
Educational Consultant
North Carolina Department
of Public Instruction
Wake Forest, NC

Some words are shown in bold, **like this.**
You can find them in the picture glossary on page 23.

Contents

What Are Your Arms and Hands?

Arms and hands are parts of your body.

Your body is made up of many parts.

Each part of your body does a job.

Arms and hands help you lift, hold, and carry.

Where Are Your Arms?

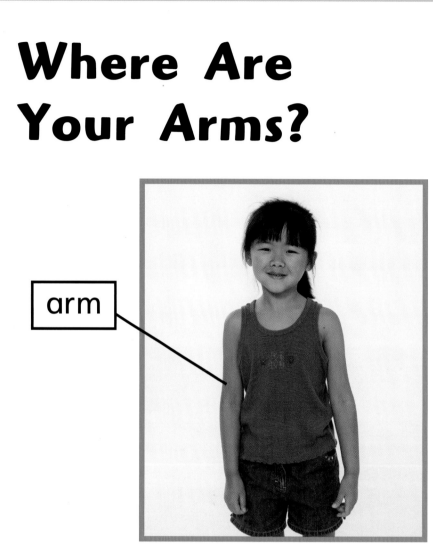

arm

Your arms rest at the sides of your body.

Your arms are joined to your body at your shoulders.

Shoulders are **joints** that help your arms move.

What Do Your Arms Look Like?

Arms look like long **tubes.**

They are covered in smooth skin.

Arms can be straight.

Arms can bend and look like the letters V or L.

What Is Inside Your Arms?

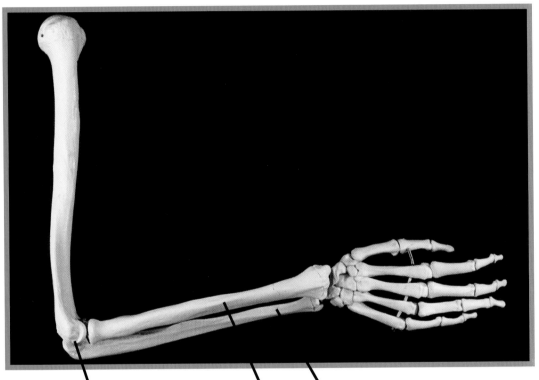

 elbow joint 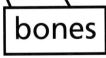 bones

Bones are inside your arms.

Your arm bones meet at your **elbow joint.**

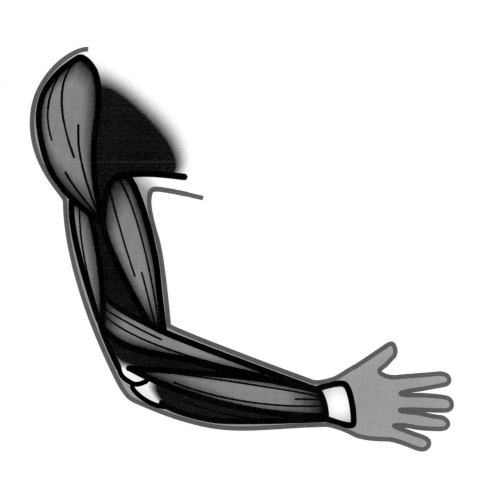

Muscles are inside your arm.

Muscles help your joints and bones move.

What Can You Do with Your Arms?

Your arms help you lift.

You can carry big things.

Your arms help you hold
your brother.

And you can hug your mom
and dad.

Where Are
Your Hands?

wrist

Your hands are at the ends
of your arms.

Wrists join your hands to
your arms.

14

Wrists are **joints** that help your hands move.

What Do Your Hands Look Like?

Hands have five fingers.

Thumbs are short, wide fingers.

Smooth skin covers hands.

Your **palm** is the soft inside of your hand.

What Is Inside Your Hands?

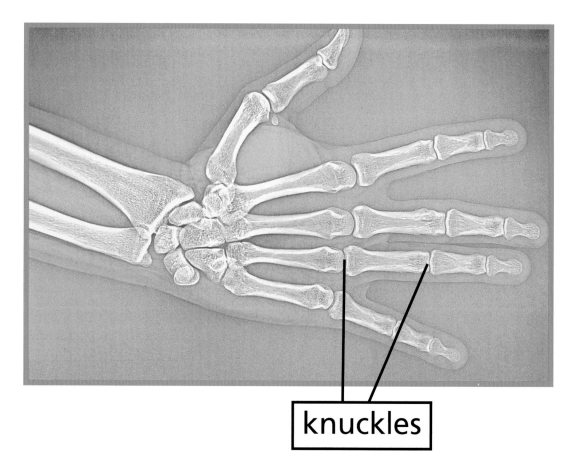

knuckles

Many **bones** are inside your hands.

Some bones fit together at **joints** called **knuckles.**

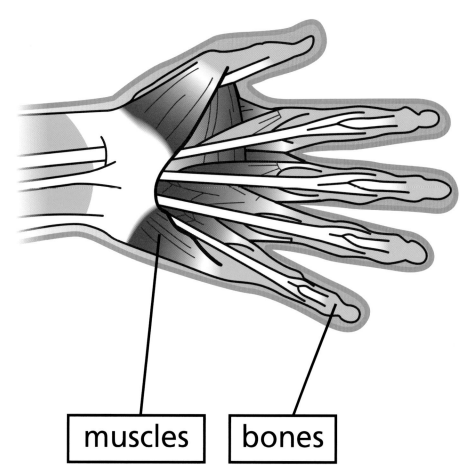

muscles | bones

Muscles help your fingers move back and forth.

They pull the bones.

What Can You Do with Your Hands?

You can touch and feel things with your hands.

You can hold another hand.

You can pick up crayons with your hands.

You can catch, hold, or carry things.

Quiz

Can you guess what these are?

Look for the answers on page 24.

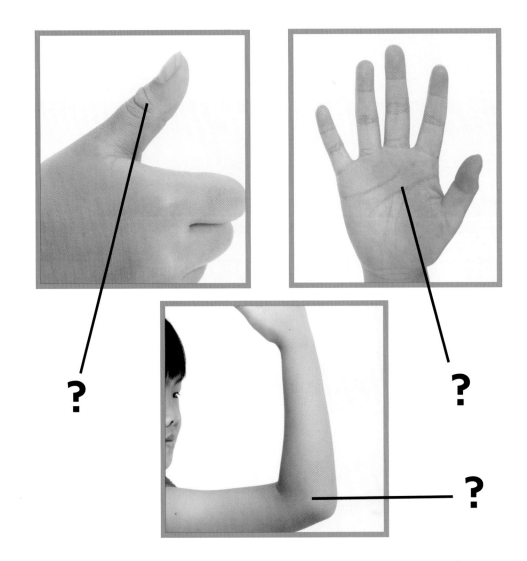

?

?

?

Picture Glossary

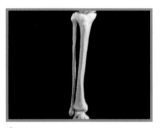

bone
pages 10, 11, 18, 19

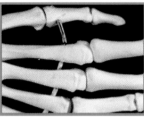

knuckle
page 18

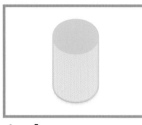

tube
page 8

elbow
page 10

muscle
pages 11, 19

wrist
pages 14, 15

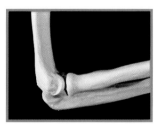

joint
pages 7, 10, 11, 15, 18

palm
page 17

Note to Parents and Teachers

Reading for information is an important part of a child's literacy development. Learning begins with a question about something. Help children think of themselves as investigators and researchers by encouraging their questions about the world around them. Each chapter in this book begins with a question. Read the question together. Look at the pictures. Talk about what you think the answer might be. Then read the text to find out if your predictions were correct. Think of other questions you could ask about the topic, and discuss where you might find the answers. Assist children in using the picture glossary and the index to practice new vocabulary and research skills.

Index

Answers to quiz on page 22

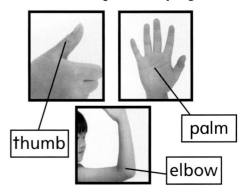

thumb

palm

elbow

24

10/03